Amazing Love

A Month of Daily Devotions for Women in Ministry

Acknowledgments

I would like to acknowledge my Lord, Jesus Christ, my first love who I absolutely adore. He has led me to write this book and continually pursues and guides me with his Amazing Love.

I would also like to thank my husband, Matt, who other than my salvation is the greatest gift I have ever received. We have grown so much together through all the adventures we have embarked on. He is my best friend, the love of my life and I cannot imagine doing any of this without him.

To my four children, Taylor, Triston, Emily, and Sarah Beth, my son-in-law Thomas, and my new grand baby, Elizabeth Rose, all of who have been so wonderful and always bring a smile to my face.

I would also like to thank Kim Yates who assisted me in finally putting all these thoughts down in paper.

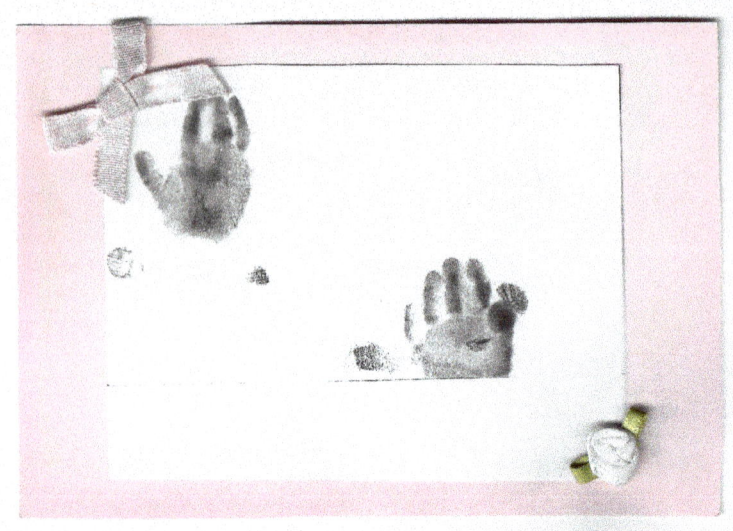

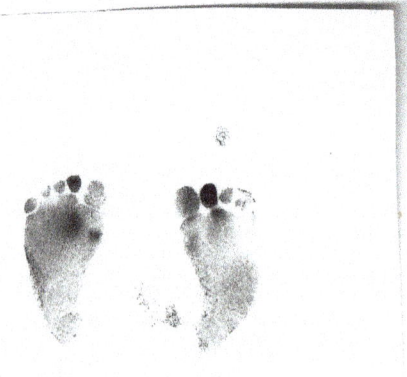

Sarah Beth Collins

In honor of Sarah Beth,
who is forever at rest in the loving arms of her savior.

(2016 ⌒ 2016)

Emily Collins

Day 1

Are You Born Again?

"Jesus replied, "Very truly I tell you, no one can see the kingdom of God unless they are born again." John 3:3

Deeper reading: John 3:1-21

If someone were to ask you to describe a memorable moment, what would it be? The human mind is amazing, and human memory is a fascinating subject. Why is it that we can't remember what we wore last week or ate for dinner three nights ago, but can remember every detail of an event that occurred 10, 20, or 30 years ago? For instance, I can remember distinctly the smell of the nurse's hands reeking of smoke as I leaned over for them to give me an epidural during the birth of my daughter and many other details of that experience even though it happened many years ago. No doubt, many women will be able to tell you distinct memories about the birth of their child and that's because that event made a huge impact on them emotionally, physically, and mentally. For me, the memorable that is engrained in my memory was the moment that I was born again.

My parents had lived in Hawaii a decade before this event while my dad was in the army. They lived there for three years and wanted to take us (their children) back to visit. So, when I was ten years old, my parents took us to the beautiful island of Hawaii for vacation. I will forever remember the deep blue color of that water and the way it sparkled as the sunlight was reflected off its surface. That Sunday, while still on the island, my family attended the church that my parents used to be members of when they lived there a decade before. During the invitation, at the end of the church service, I felt this overwhelming tug at my heart. I knew that I needed to walk the aisle to give my life to Christ.

The fear of walking to the front of that church in front of all those strangers was real and overwhelming, but the fear of the Lord was stronger. I tried to get to my mom so she could walk with me, but my brother, who was sitting right next to me, stuck his leg up so I couldn't get through to my mom. There is no doubt now that Satan was placing roadblocks in my way to keep me from that alter, but the draw of my Savior was strong. Because I could not get to my mom, I instead grabbed my dad's hand who was sitting right by me, and he walked down the aisle with me. When I reached the front, I talked to the pastor and surrendered my being, my soul, and my life to Christ. I remember feeling so clean and could not wait to tell everyone when I got back home to Tennessee.

Today, when I talk to other people, I will often come across those who cannot tell me the moment that they were born again. I hear things like," I said a prayer when I was little," or "I have been going to church my whole life," or" I have always believed in God." But the memory of their salvation is not clear--it is not distinct, not transformative. My husband always does a good job of explaining it like this. "You remember the moment that you were married, right? You will never forget that day, it was special to you." Significant events leave us with significant memories. Our salvation is the MOST significant event of one's life. It was a time when you entered into a covenant relationship with Christ and I promise if you have truly been born again, you will remember that moment without a shadow of doubt.

Reflection

If you have been born again, take some time today to reflect on that day, that moment that your life was forever changed. Dwell on those memories and share that story with someone else. Thank God for his salvation and the sacrifice that He made for you. If you cannot remember the moment that you were born again, then you need to ask yourself if you truly have received salvation. Remember, God sent His one and only Son to die on the cross for our sins and three days later, he rose from the grave to conquer death. Salvation can only come through Him. He wants everyone to have this gift of salvation and doesn't wish for anyone to perish, but we must willingly accept His gift.

I pray that if you are struggling with knowing if you are truly born again that God will convict your heart and lead you to kneel before him, confess your sins, and believe in Him. I have known missionaries, pastors', pastors' wives, and Bible College students who realized they were not truly born again. Please don't let pride stand in your way. Tomorrow is not given.

Day 2

My Lost Friend

"But you will receive power when the Holy Spirit comes on you; and you will be my witnesses in Jerusalem, and in all Judea and Samaria, and to the ends of the earth." Acts 1:8

Deeper Reading: Acts 16:6-10

What fills you with compassion? When you see orphans or children in need, it usually fills us with an overwhelming burden to want to do something to help them, right? It's the same for me when I think about people who have never had a chance to hear the good news of Jesus Christ. It fills me with such compassion, and I want to do whatever it takes to get the gospel to them. Paul also was filled with compassion to take the gospel to places where it had never been. In the book of Acts, Paul had a vision of a Macedonia man. Paul was trying to go somewhere else but the Holy Spirit redirected him through a vision to go and share the good news of Jesus Christ to someone who had never heard before.

I was sitting in my drafty living room one fall afternoon in the parsonage where we lived. My husband was the pastor of a church in rural Southwest Virginia. Everything was quiet that afternoon: my baby and toddler were taking a nap and my nine-year-old was in her room playing quietly. I had been feeling for months God stirring in our hearts to do something internationally. I had been praying without ceasing asking God for direction and just waiting on Him. Waiting on God is not always easy because we want Him to answer us right away.

That afternoon as I sat in my living room praying and crying out to God about it, I had a vision of a woman dressed in African clothing but her face was a blur. I immediately became broken for this woman because I knew that she needed to hear the good news of Jesus Christ. I remember telling God, whatever I had to sacrifice and whatever I had to do, would He please get me to this woman. I know some of you are thinking, she saw a vision? Believe me, I had my doubts about it also. That same day I wrote in my journal what had happened and I also prayed that God would put someone in my husbands' path (while he was at Bible College taking classes) that would point us in the right direction of where God was leading us to go internationally. I had not said anything to my husband about this vision. When I went to pick him up from classes the next day, he started to tell me about an opportunity in West Africa that got put in his path yesterday for us to go serve for a semester. I said, "well, let me tell you about what has happened to me." I was still trying to process it all. All I knew was that I was broken for this woman to hear the gospel and I was going to do whatever it took to get to her. I knew it was of God because of the brokenness of her needing to hear the gospel.

Reflection

Are you broken for the lost? Are you broken for the ones who have never had a chance to hear before? If so, ask God to make a way and put you where you need to be, when you need to be there. If not, ask God to burden your heart for someone that needs to hear the gospel and that He will put that person in your path or send you to them.

Julie Collins

Day 3

That's Not an Idol!

"Yet I hold this against you: You have forsaken the love you had at first." Revelation 2:4

Deeper Reading: Revelation 2:1-7

When we think of idols, especially when we are reading through the Old Testament, we usually think of a golden calf or a statue, right? Well, although these things can most certainly be idols, idols can also come in many different forms. It can be sports, money, kids, spouses, time, jobs, self, and anything else that may keep us from deepening our relationship with Christ. An idol can be ANYTHING that we put above our love of God.

Many years ago, I was reading through the book of Jeremiah, and I thought, "Why can't these Israelites get it? Why do they keep having idols and not making God their first love?" And like He often does, the Holy Spirit made it clear to me that I too had an idol, and it wasn't a golden calf or some kind of statue, but instead it was my husband. How can my husband be an idol you ask? I was carving out time for my husband daily to spend time with him and serve him. I was not doing that with God. I only spent a few hours a week with Him. Instead of putting God first, He was simply getting the leftovers and my husband was at the center of my life. God is a jealous God, and he wanted that place in my life that I was reserving only for my husband. Christ loves us with an agape love, a love that is unconditional, sacrificial highest form of love. I thought, "I can't love you like that, God." In Jeremiah 3:14, God refers to himself as Israels' husband and He wanted to have that place in my life too. He wanted, and still does, to be my first love. I had to repent in my living room as the Holy Spirit convicted me, and I asked him to forgive me of the idol that I was putting before him.

A lot of times, I would look to my husband to fulfill a need for me to feel beautiful. He has always made me feel like a gorgeous woman but if he didn't notice me one day when I needed to be noticed, it would just crush me. When Christ became my first love and I removed the idol (my

5

husband), I stood in front of the mirror in my bedroom for the very first time and felt beautiful because my God, my love, formed me in the womb. He designed me, desires me, and longs to be with me. He is the greatest love that I have ever known. He is my first love.

Reflection

Take some time to think about your own life. What idols do you have in your life? Ask the Holy Spirit to search you and bring to mind any idols that are keeping Him from being your first love. Just repent and experience God being your first love.

"Love the LORD your God with all your heart and with all your soul and with all your strength. These commandments that I give you today are to be on your hearts."

Deuteronomy 6:5-6

Day 4

A Date with God

But when you pray, go into your room, close the door and pray to your Father, who is unseen. Then your Father, who sees what is done in secret, will reward you. Matthew 6:6

Deeper Reading: Matthew 6: 5-15

Do you have a good relationship with someone that you never talk to or spend time with? I can answer that question for you: No. It is hard to have an intimate and close relationship with someone that you never communicate with. It's also hard to have a good relationship with the lord if you never talk to Him.

I cherish walks with my husband. It is a time that we can have uninterrupted conversations and time alone with just us. It helps me to feel very connected to him in this busyness of life. We have to make sure that we are being intentional about spending that time together or something will always try to steal that time away from us. It is the same with our relationship with God. He wants to spend time alone with you. He desires to talk, listen, and just be with you. My favorite time of day is right after lunch. When my children were little, it was nap time. I would lay my children down in their bed and it would give me the opportunity to spend some time with God.

Now, that my children are older, they no longer take naps, but we have still continued the tradition as we all have our quiet time after lunch. They know that it is mom's time with the Lord, and they should not interrupt. I find my favorite spot (which is on the back porch) and just have time with Him. I journal, which has become my prayer journal where I pour my heart out, and write down scripture that the Lord has spoken to me that day. I read in His Word, listen to worship music, and sometimes I just sit very quiet in His presence. It is honestly my favorite time of day. I guard it like I guard a date with my husband. His love for me captivates me and I cherish this time of intimacy with the Lord.

Reflection

Do you want to grow in your relationship and intimacy with the Lord? If you don't currently have alone time with the Lord, set aside time to do that. It looks different for everyone. Mine is in the middle of the day when I am fully awake and the house is quiet. My husband has had some of his greatest intimate moments with the Lord as he was driving down the interstate. Just find time to sacrifice to Him.

Do you already have a time with the Lord? I want to encourage you to guard it and think of it like an important meeting or date, so something or someone will not steal that from you. You can do different things to keep it fresh. Some days you may want to add in worship music or take a walk in His creation. We like to do different things on dates with our spouses, so do different things with your alone time with the Lord. Make sure it doesn't become something to check off your checklist but is instead something you look forward to each day.

Day 5

A Don't Want to Serve That Way!

"Just as the Son of Man did not come to be served, but to serve, and to give his life as a ransom for many." Matthew 20:28

Deeper Reading: Matthew 20: 20-28

When you think of serving, what comes to your mind? For me, I think of my Mama Dot, (Grandmother) who was always serving those around her for no reward of her own. She was constantly giving of herself to serve others. It seemed to come so easy for her. For me, I feel like a two-year-old sometimes who is throwing a fit on the Walmart floor when God asks me to serve somewhere that I don't want to.

One vivid instance of this happening in my life was when I was asked to serve in the 2-year-old class at church. For some people, that would be no problem, but for me it was. I am a stay-at-home mom and homeschooling mom, and I was with my children all day, every day. I longed to be around adults and to be able to minister to those with whom I could have conversations with and relate to. I had been praying for God to show me where to serve within the church, and the last place that I wanted to be was with the two-year-olds in the nursery. That was not my vision of serving that "I" wanted to do. Then one Sunday during my husband's sermon, which was on serving the body of Christ, the Holy Spirit confirmed in my heart, that is exactly where He wanted me to serve. He reminded me that I am here to serve and not be served. I remember asking God, "Why would you ask me to do this, when you know I need a break from kids?" The Spirit reminded me that Jesus left His throne in Heaven to come to earth to serve and not be served. My service was not about what I needed, it is what God needed me to do and be. When we serve, we need to understand that we should not expect anything in return and that we need to take the focus off of us. It was a small step of surrender and obedience of less of me and more of Him. That is my reward, that through surrendering to His will, I was becoming more like Him.

Reflection

Are you currently serving in your church or in a specific ministry? If not, have you asked God to show you where He wants you to serve others? Do you need to surrender less of you so you can have more of Him?

If you are serving, ask God to reveal to you how your service can reflect Him more: is God calling you to serve in a different way? Does your attitude towards ministry need to change to better reflect the type of service God expects of us? Do you simply need to pray that God opens doors and allows you to reach further in your ministry?

I Have Helping Hands.

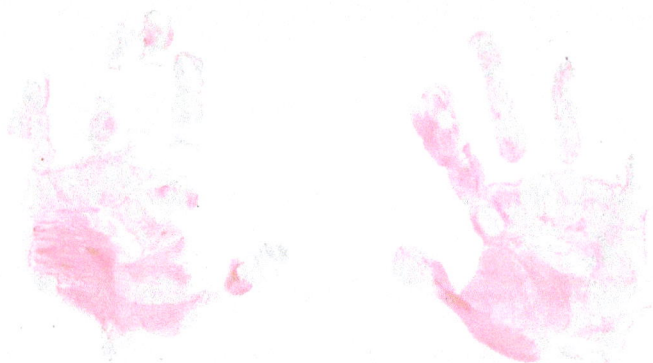

Love and Service go hand in hand.
Thank you God For Making My Hands.

Emily Collins

Day 6

How Will God Ever Do That?

Joshua told the people, "Consecrate yourselves, for tomorrow the LORD will do amazing things among you." Joshua 3:5

Deeper Reading: Joshua 3

In modern day Christianity, the concept of faith is often talked about and referenced, but rarely understood. What does it mean to have "faith" and how does this idea relate to our Christian walk? God tells us that it is impossible to please Him without faith, and according to the Oxford Dictionary, faith is defined as complete trust or confidence in someone or something.

One big step of faith for my family is when my husband and I went on our first vision trip to West Africa and God confirmed to us that He wanted us to go back. He wanted us to return as a family for a semester to a specific village so we could share the gospel. I would be taking my children to an unknown place and they would be stripped of everything they knew. My children at the time were ten, three, and one. We also had to raise twenty thousand dollars in six months. That amount of money seemed like twenty million to us. My husband was a full time Bible student making minimum wage working on campus at the Bible College and I stayed at home and had no income. We literally lived off one hundred and twenty dollars a week for our family of five, so we certainly didn't have our own money to use. In those six months though, we saw what only God could do. We shared how we felt God leading us to go and watched with amazement at how God provided. We had churches from all over the southeast United States that would take up love offerings or take us on for monthly support. In those six months, God provided every bit of money that we needed to go to Africa for a semester. It took complete faith for us to trust and make plans to go to Africa for a semester and not have a clue where the money was going to come from.

Reflection

Is there a huge obstacle standing in your way? Just like the Israelites trusted God when crossing over the Jordan, we need to trust Him for whatever obstacle that we may be standing in our way. Remember it is impossible to please God without faith.

"Is anything too hard for the Lord?"

Genesis 18:14

Day 7

When Life is a Blur

"He says, "Be still, and know that I am God…" Psalm 46:10

Deeper reading: Psalm 46

Is there news that you hear that just comes unexpectedly? When we hear that unexpected news, it just shocks us to our core. That is exactly what happened one Sunday afternoon in the middle of summer of 2012.

I had just laid my baby down for a nap in the pack-n-play in the old farmhouse we were staying in on Sunday afternoons between the morning and afternoon services at church. I received a phone call right after I laid my daughter down and it was my mom telling me that we better come to Tennessee quickly because she was not sure my dad was going to make it. "What?!" I had just talked to him that morning and he told me that he loved me. Now that I think about it, dad never called on Sunday mornings because he knew what a busy morning that was for us in ministry. We grabbed the kids in what seemed like record speed and got in the car and headed to Tennessee. On the way, I was praying for God to let me have a chance to say good-bye to my dad one last time.

Then another phone call came in from my mom. My husband pulled over on the side of the road while we were still in Virginia. I heard the words that no 32-year-old wants to hear. She said, "Julie, he's gone." I remember the only thing I could do was cry out and for the remainder of the trip and for many weeks after, I only felt numbness. That was the absolute longest car ride of my life.

On the way back to Tennessee, I looked up in the sky and there was a beautiful rainbow that felt like it was exactly for me. I felt God's peace and comfort through His creation. During this time, we had many unknowns. Did we need to move back to Tennessee to help my mom? Should we still move to Africa as we had been called to do? While all these things captivated my thoughts, the Holy Spirit reminded me of this verse: *"Be still and know that I am God."*

Reflection

Do you ever feel that life is too much and it even can cause you to feel numb at times? Do you ever wonder what God is doing? I want to speak this same verse over you today that He spoke over me when I was full of fear and trying to figure things out for myself, "Be Still and know that I am God." This psalm was written in a time of war and "Be Still" means to "stop fighting", "stop fearing", and acknowledge who your God is.

Taylor Collins Schnitzler

Day 8

Don't Worry

"But seek first his kingdom and his righteousness, and all these things will be given to you as well. Therefore do not worry about tomorrow, for tomorrow will worry about itself. Each day has enough trouble of its own." Matthew 6: 33-34

Deeper Reading: Matthew 6:25-34

Worrying can cause so much grief on a person. According to The Oxford Dictionary, worry is defined in the following way: to give way to anxiety or unease; allow one's mind to dwell on difficulty or troubles. When I choose to worry about things, it literally makes me physically sick. Why is it so hard for us to trust God and not worry about things?

One of the most worrisome times in my life was when we were raising funds to go live in Africa for a semester. We had a church that was a few hours away that wanted us to come share about our vision. We literally had enough money to put gas in our car to get up there to the church that we were supposed to speak at and that was it. We had no money for food to go out to eat (which was what they wanted to do that night) and absolutely no money for gas to get home. We stepped out in faith and trusted God. When we got to the city that evening, the pastor said they wanted to take us out to eat and pay for it. What a blessing! I am not going to lie, I was a little worried how we were going to be able to get gas for the way home or even be able to get our family of five food for the next day.

We presented at the church that day and the church felt led to support our mission to Africa. They were going to take up a love offering for the next four months. We were so excited but in the back of my mind, I was still wondering how we were getting home and how we were going to eat. Right after service, the pastor said, "I want to take your car to the gas station and fill it up before you leave." Then, I had a lady approach me and tell me about a beautiful rainbow that was shining through the window when I was sharing. She also handed me thirty dollars. We now had money to buy food for the way home.

As fallen humans, we like to think we are in control and when things seem out of our hands, we tend to worry and stress instead of leaning on and trusting the promises God has made to us. Faith and worry are contrary to one another; they are diametrically opposed. God makes it clear that He will take care of our every need when we are seeking His kingdom first. That is the promise we must lean on and let go of the rest.

Reflection

Why do we worry about things that God tells us not to worry about? Do you have something that you are worried or concerned about today? Take it to God, and watch Him take care of you in ways that you have never could have dreamed up on your own. Just remember, seek first His kingdom and His righteousness and all these things will be added into you.

"Trust in the LORD with all your heart and lean not on your own understanding; in all your ways submit to him, and he will make your paths straight."

Proverbs 3:5-6

Day 9

Please Put Someone in My Path!

"How, then, can they call on the one they have not believed in? And how can they believe in the one of whom they have not heard? And how can they hear without someone preaching to them?" Romans 10:14-15

Deeper Reading: Romans 10

Have you ever asked God to put someone in your path so you could have a chance to share with them the good news of Jesus Christ? Sometimes, it is so hard for people to get out of their comfort zones and share the gospel with others. We are always afraid of what others might think and that we may offend someone. I too have those same thoughts but I am reminded of Jesus words to us in Acts 1:8; "But you will receive power when the Holy Spirit comes on you, and you will be my witnesses in Jerusalem, and in all Judea and Samaria, and to the ends of the earth." I love to share the gospel with others and I prayed for five months that God would put someone in my path who needed to hear it. I started praying in August of 2012 and the Lord put someone in my path the end of December 2012.

I was standing in line at Walmart with my one-year-old daughter, Emily. This was before the times of self-checkout lines. There was a lady behind me with a baby the same age. We began to talk as we shared things in common with both our children being around the same age. We said good-bye, nice to meet you, and went on our different ways. A few weeks later, I was once again standing in the Walmart line with my one-year-old. The exact same girl with her child from a few weeks ago was standing in line behind me again. Like, how does that even happen? We both started chit chatting again, and we were both a little bewildered at how we ended up in the exact same line together again. When I left Walmart, I was so convicted by the Holy Spirit because I didn't share anything with her about the Lord. I was also reminded that I had been praying for God to put someone in my path. I was discouraged because I thought I had missed an opportunity to share the gospel. Then one Sunday morning a lady who usually kept the nursery asked if I would fill in for her that day. As I was welcoming the babies into the nursery, there stood a new face with her child. But it really wasn't a new face to me because it was the same girl that God had put in my path in the Walmart checkout line two different times in the past month. As you can imagine, we were both astonished. This time, I asked her if she would like to get lunch some time. She accepted and we went to a local restaurant a few days later. As we sat in conversation, I shared with her the good news of Jesus Christ. The verse that captivated her heart was John 3:16. She thought about the love she had for her own son and she wanted to experience a love that was so great that God would send His one and only son so we could have a way to heaven. She asked Jesus to come into her life that day and she was a new creation.

It is so important that we pray and ask God for people to share with and also for us to step outside our comfort zones and be obedient to the command that Jesus gave us. This could have been a missed opportunity if I chose to think of only myself.

Reflection

Have you had times when God has put people in your path that need to hear the good news of Jesus? If not, ask Him to put those people in your path or to send you to those people. I promise you, He will answer that prayer. He wants no one to perish but wants all to have everlasting life.

Day 10

Isolated

"Leave here, turn eastward and hide in the Kerith Ravine, east of the Jordan." 1 Kings 17:3

Deeper Reading: 1 Kings 17-19

In 1 Kings 17:3, God is telling Elijah to go to Cherith for a season of separation for his spiritual journey that God was preparing for him. We all need to have these seasons of preparation for our spiritual journey. Most of the time we think of the word isolation as having a negative connotation. We think of it along with words like lonely, alone, frustration. And though isolation can sometimes be this way, it is exactly what God may need us to go through so He can prepare us for our journey with Him.

There was a church in southwestern Virginia that called my husband to pastor about 4 years after we had been called into ministry. This would be my husband's second pastorate. For my husband to take the position, it meant we needed to move off the Bible College campus where we were living at the time. The church had a parsonage on its property, and it was literally in the middle of nowhere. The nearest Walmart was 30 minutes away. We could not afford internet, cable, and definitely no cell phone except a pre-paid cell phone for emergencies. We knew only the people in our church. It was a very isolating place for us.

During this time of being stripped of all modern-day distractions, I fell in love the Lord. He truly became my first love. I had no Facebook to distract me and no television to watch, so I spent my extra time that I would have been doing those things and spent them with the Lord and in his Word. It was a time of personal revival for me. Even though it was one of the hardest years in ministry for us, I look back on it as one of the sweetest times that I have ever had with the Lord. Just like married couples know that it is important for them to get away together so they can have time with just the two of them because they know that it will help their relationship, it is the same with our relationship with God. Sometimes, God needs to take us to a place of isolation so we can grow in our relationship together.

Reflection

Are you in an isolating place right now? During this time, you can have many questions. Use this time to grow in your relationship with the Lord instead of focusing on the negative things that maybe bothering you about the isolating place. Maybe, you need to go to an isolating place for a while so you can spend time with just you and the Lord. Maybe you need to strip things out of your life so you can work on your relationship with the Lord. All relationships need time together and time where they can just focus on one another.

Emily Collins

Day 11

Take Me to the Village!

"…the LORD your God is giving you, a land flowing with milk and honey, just as the LORD, the God of your ancestors, promised you."
Deuteronomy 27:3

Deeper Reading: Deuteronomy 27-28

Many times when God calls us into ministry or calls us to do something, we expect it to automatically be a "land flowing of milk and honey." We expect Him to have the kinks worked out and for everything to be simple and easy. However, ministry is not easy. It is messy and difficult and we often have to struggle to get to the place God intends for us to be.

Before we arrived in Africa for our semester there, I was excited. I just knew that God was going to use me and my family in a big way, and I had visions of just how this was going to work. However, after a month in, I was ready to go home. Our family of five was staying with a single male missionary, and you could just imagine how that was going. He also was still learning the language and was not at a place where he could share the gospel in the heart language of the people group we were working with. I remember thinking, "Why are we here, this is not somewhere I just want to be for a vacation. This wasn't how I envisioned our ministry being. Our goal was to share the gospel and it seemed like there were so many obstacles in the way preventing that from happening.

During this time of struggle, our family knew that we were supposed to be involved in this one particular village on the beach. We found a house to rent in that village on the coast of West Africa. Could this be our land flowing with milk and honey? From the outside, it certainly didn't appear this way. First, the house had no running water, no electricity, and no furniture. We would have to walk 3 miles one way to the market to get food. We would also have no car or cell phone reception in the village. Finally, the biggest problem was we had no "mouthpiece" to help us share the gospel. On the outside, this looked worse than our current situation. Was this really God's promise? But as we were praying about this decision, God provided us with a sign that this land would be fruitful for us if we just trusted Him. God provided that mouthpiece miraculously. He put that man (mouthpiece), in my husbands' path while he was in the market getting clothes made. My husband was able to lead him to the Lord and he moved out to the village with us for my husband to disciple him and he became our mouthpiece. With this huge obstacle out of the way, we knew God would provide for us in those minor areas, too. This opened our eyes to better see how this land was flowing with milk and honey and we were so excited to see the blessings God had in store for us and for the people in this Islamic Village.

Reflection

Is there something that God may be calling you to do? He desires a heart of obedience and wants to take you to a place flowing with milk and honey. Sometimes, following God will take you out of your comfort zone so you can rely on Him for everything. The Israelites were trusting God to cross over the Jordan River and God wants us to walk in faith and obedience so He can take us to a land flowing with milk and honey.

"In you, LORD my God, I put my trust."

Psalm 25:1

Day 12

The Harvest

"The harvest is plentiful but the workers are few." Luke 10:2

Deeper Reading: Luke 10; 1 Corinthians 3

Have you ever planted a garden? Gardening is not easy. It's a full-time job that lasts from early spring to late fall. The first steps occur early in the spring when you have to plow the ground to prepare it for seeds. Then, you have to plant. This can be meticulous work. During the summer you have to be sure to water and weed it to protect those new plants. And in fall you have to prepare to harvest. Each job is so very important but my favorite is always the harvest. I love to see the fruit of the labor.

When we followed God in obedience and moved to the village, we saw an amazing harvest of souls. When we went to live in the village we lived just like the others in the village. We washed our clothes in buckets and drew our water up from the well everyday just like they did. God gives you what you need to do the work He has called you to do. When we started making relationships and getting to know the others in our village who were born into Islam, we learned that seeds were planted years before when other missionaries went through the village. One of the ladies that I was able to lead to Christ told me that when she was a little girl, she had heard someone talk about Jesus on the cross, but she had waited for years for someone to come back and explain it to her. That opened my eyes so much about there being a huge harvest but not enough workers. She had waited over ten years for someone to explain the good news of Jesus Christ to her. We all have a job to do. It may be plowing the ground, it may be planting seeds, or it may be to reap the harvest. One thing is for sure, we need more workers.

Reflection

God tells us that the Harvest is plentiful, but the workers are few. Have you prayed and asked God to send you?   Maybe you are needed for plowing, planting, watering, or for the harvest. He needs workers for His garden; pray that there would be more workers for His kingdom.

"But you will receive power when the Holy Spirit comes on you; and you will be my witnesses in Jerusalem, and in all Judea and Samaria, and to the ends of the earth."

Acts 1:8

Day 13

When I Am Weak, He is Strong

"He gives strength to the weary and increases the power of the weak."
Isaiah 40:29

Deeper Reading: Isaiah 40: 29-31

Have you ever been so tired that you just felt you couldn't go on? When we lived in China, we hiked straight up a mountain in our city. I have never seen so many stairs in my life! About halfway through, I thought to myself, "I just want to quit. I cannot go on any longer." But something inside of me just wouldn't let my legs stop moving. I managed to persevere, and climbed to the top experiencing the gorgeous view! It can be the same way in our spiritual walk with the Lord. We can become exhausted in our walk, but we must persevere.

We had been living in the village in West Africa for months with no running water, electricity, different sicknesses, and the list goes on. It was our last day in the village before we were leaving to come back to the United States. I was exhausted mentally, spiritually, physically, and emotionally. Stick a fork in me, I was done. I also was struggling with doubt because I had not met the woman that God broke my heart for a couple of years before through a vision. I told God that whatever I had to do, get me to this woman so I can share with her the most amazing love I have ever known.

Before we were to leave, I had one last opportunity to share with a group of ladies. We were going to be showing a movie about Jesus. I was exhausted and, just like halfway up that mountain in China, I was ready to just throw in the towel. I scrambled all the energy I could and my daughter Taylor and I, went to the village t to share the gospel one last time.

After the film, there was one woman who wanted to walk with me as I ventured back to my village. When we were in the woods and there was nobody around, she started asking me questions about the film. She was a Muslim but wanted to know about "my Jesus". I told her about Jesus and she believed and she prayed right there in her own language to receive Christ as her Savior. At that moment, the Holy Spirit said, Julie, this is the woman that you had the vision for 2 years ago, the one you were so broken for and who needed the gospel. Looking back on this experience, I am so glad I did not give up. It was not only a life-changing experience for that woman in the woods, it was a life changing experience for me. It revealed to me that I am weak. I can depend on his strength to get me through.

Reflection

Do you ever get to a point in your spiritual journey where you are just tired? You feel like you just can't go on? Remember, that when we are weak, He is strong. Pray and ask God to help you to persevere.

Triston Collins

Day 14

When God Redirects Our Path

"In my distress I called to the Lord, and he answered me. From deep in the realm of the dead I called for help, and you listened to my cry."
Jonah 2:1-2

Deeper Reading: Jonah 1-4

Has God ever redirected your path or told you to do something that you just did not want to do? Has he told you to wait because He wanted you to do something else first? This is always a tough test of our faith. As humans, we have a deep desire to be in control and to do things how and when we want. But the Bible continually teaches us that we are so short-sighted. God has infinite wisdom and knows what is best for us. The best thing we can do is get out of the way and let God.

When we got back from our semester in West Africa, we were sure that God wanted us to go straight back overseas. We knew this was what He called us to do. He had confirmed it in His word, our hearts, and we had total peace that God was going to use us overseas. Then the unthinkable happened. He shut the door and told us to do something that we did not want to do. He wanted us to church plant in America. Oh, how I struggled with this and mourned it like a death. I wanted to live among people who have never had chance to hear the gospel before. Instead, God was telling us to stay in a country where the people had every chance to hear the gospel, but over and over, they chose to reject it.

I know what some of you are thinking, especially if you have never been overseas to an unreached people group. I understand there are many lost people in America, but they do have many opportunities to hear the gospel or seek someone who could share with them. Just like Jonah didn't want to go to the Ninevites, I definitely didn't want to stay in the southeastern United States. I wanted to be somewhere where churches and believers were few and far between, but that was not God's plan and we realized that His plan would always be better than ours. So, the Lord opened up an opportunity for us to begin our church planting in the northern United States. This was hard, but when we submitted and obeyed, He put the desire in our hearts to church plant in the U.S.

Reflection

When God redirects our path and plans it can just hurt. Has God redirected you or told you to do something opposite to what you wanted or desired? It's honestly hard when this happens but we must understand that God loves us more than anything or anyone. He has a purpose for us and we are just to submit and be obedient. When we align our hearts with God, His desires will be our desires. Pray that God shows you where you are supposed to be and that you have the faith to trust Him.

"The LORD is good to those whose hope is in him, to the one who seeks him;"

Lamentations 3:25

Day 15

I Will Not Quit. I Will Persevere!

"If God is for us, who can be against us?" Romans 8:31

Deeper Reading: Romans 8:38-39

Has someone ever done something to you that wounded you so badly you thought you would never recover? As Christians, we expect to be mistreated, misjudged, and hurt by those outside our faith, but sometimes the worst hurt can come from other Christians. This is what many call "church hurt." Church hurt is incredibly painful and often difficult to overcome, but God can tech us lessons and bring us closer to Him through any type of circumstance or situation.

After we returned from Africa, my husband worked as a mission's intern. During this time, our spirits became troubled with some of the actions our lead pastor was doing. We prayed for a long time how to approach the situation in love and trust. A whirlwind happened after my husband felt led to talk to him about these concerns. The pastor's vehement denial of his actions led to swift defamation of our integrity and reputation.

We knew God was calling us to plant a church in America. After months of prayer, he called us to another state to plant this church. We went to this new state trusting that God would provide the vision for the new plant, work for my husband, and a home for us. As we waited for the Lord to show us and give us vision, we worked with another church planter in the area. We told him our intentions all along. God also provided a home and work for my husband at the post office. It wasn't long after we were there that God did show us the city where He wanted us to plant. It would be about 45 minutes away from our current location and we were excited that God had given us such a clear vision. Then the unthinkable happened. We were told by the "church planter' who had always seemed a little insecure and was even struggling in his church plant that we were not welcomed back to his church anymore. We were like, "what just happened?" We found out that "the church planter" made a phone call to our old pastor who we had just caught in lies. Before we knew it, we had hurtful, outrageous lies spreading about us like wildfire. There was not one ounce of truth to any of them but they were spreading fast and totally out of our control. The "church planter" even called people at the state and national level telling them not to have anything to do with us. You could honestly see the enemy trying to stop all our efforts and make us give up. The battle seemed so severe and I was so deeply wounded that I didn't want to continue on this journey of following the Lord.

I remember being in the shower crying out to God that this was all too much and I just couldn't continue in ministry. Satan had seemingly won and there was nothing I could do about it. Then God quickly reminded me of Romans 8:38-39, *"For I am convinced that neither death nor life, neither angels nor demons, neither the present nor the future, nor any powers, neither height nor depth, nor anything else in all creation, will be able to separate us from the love of God that is in Christ Jesus our Lord."* I was convicted of the fact that I was not in ministry for me and nothing I was doing was about me. I was His, and I was here to do His work and no power of man or scheme of the enemy could separate me from Christ.

God gave us a vision of the church plant that He wanted us to do. All we had to do then was put our faith in Him, follow His direction for our lives, and put aside everything else. God did utilize us to plant a church with that vision. That church has led countless souls to Jesus and is involved in His mission worldwide. Not even the worst schemes of men or Satan can stop the will of God in the lives of those who love him and are called according to His purpose.

Reflection

Has someone or something wounded you so badly that you thought you couldn't move forward. I want to encourage you to keep pressing forward when it hurts, when its unbearable. We need to remind ourselves that what God has called us to do is not about us, our comforts, what makes us happy, or any glory for ourselves. It is about our desire to be more like Him and to follow Him wherever that may lead us. Conversely, can you think back to a time when you were the one causing the hurt? Even if that hurt wasn't intentional or in malice, ask God to forgive you and if possible, reach out to those you may have harmed. Attempt to mend that relationship and make things right.

Day 16

The God of Hope

"What no eye has seen, what no ear has heard, and what no human mind has conceived, the things God has prepared for those who love him." 1 Corinthians 2:9

Deeper Reading: Romans 15:13; Galatians 6:9

What comes to your mind when you think of the word, hope? It is defined as a feeling of expectation and desire for a certain thing to happen. In the terrible "storm" that brought us back to Tennessee to plant the church God had given us the vision for, this verse was sent to me when I was feeling completely hopeless. *"What no eye has seen, what no ear has heard, and what no human mind has conceived, the things God has prepared for those who love him."* (1 Corinthians 2:9.)

While we were in Michigan, the Lord gave us a vision for the type of church that He wanted us to plant. He wanted it to be an Acts 1:8 church and a church that would reach the unreached. He also gave us a vision for a building in a downtown area and we could even see the brick on the wall. He wanted this building to not just be a place where they used it to meet it corporately but to use the building as a ministry that would reach out to the community. So, when we first starting gathering to meet in Tennessee, we would meet in someone's house or in the public park. I am not going to lie, there were times when I thought how will God bring this vision about. "Is anything too hard for the LORD?"

Two years into the church plant, there were lots of struggles and lots of questions but the Lord continued to work and before we knew it, we were sitting in a building downtown where you could see the brick on the wall. There was a ministry that the building was used for called Café Agape. It was a coffee house style opened on Friday and Saturday nights with live Christian bands playing. We were reaching the unchurched and unreached. My favorite is that God led us to an unreached people group in the Philippines that our church plant partnered with. To this day, they are still going to this people group to share the gospel. So, when I feel hopeless or wonder how things are going to happen, I remember this time.

Amazing Love

It feels my heart with such joy to remember how He has been so faithful.

Reflection

When and if you have those times of feeling hopeless, remember the things He has done and the things that He has in store for those who love Him. He is our hope!

Day 17

The Battle is Real

"Be alert and of sober mind. Your enemy the devil prowls around like a roaring lion looking for someone to devour." 1 Peter 5:8

Deeper Reading: Ephesians 6:10-20

Do you realize that there is always a battle happening between God and his enemy? Even this very second, good and evil are colliding, battling for the souls of the people here on earth. For those of us who are Christians, we are part of God's army, but satan is always attempting to cause pain and destruction, even to God's people. This is especially true as we begin to invade enemy territory. We faced many battles in our church planting days. You really could honestly feel the enemy trying to invade. He tried to invade my marriage. He tried to invade the lives of my children, He tried to invade our ministry. He tried to invade our home. But God tells us in His word that we are protected as long as we are "alert and of sober mind." During these times, we must draw close to Him. For me, this meant I stayed on my knees a lot for my husband and my children.

The enemy had already been hard after my husband, myself, and our character before we ever even got started, but the enemy also came after our children during this time. This is especially scary for parents because our children are incredibly vulnerable. For my children, this spiritual battle manifested itself in their sleep. For a couple of months, all three of my children kept waking up with nightmares. This one particular night they had each woken up with different things. One just couldn't sleep; one had a bad dream; the other one just needed mom for comfort. For a mother, this can be exhausting. You always think that the sleepless nights end after those early years, but this time in my life proved that wasn't true. I had just laid the youngest back down and went back to bed, and I heard my husband (who never talks in his sleep), start speaking this unknown language with great authority. I would be lying if I didn't admit that it was a bit concerning and disturbing, but I remember praying, "please God, let him remember this dream." Normally, my husband never remembers his dreams and I just knew that tonight would be no different. However, it wasn't five minutes after that that he woke up and said, "I just had the craziest dream!" He said, "I was fighting demons out of our home in the name of Jesus!" I was stunned and told him how I too had been fighting the demons from our house, just in a different way. After that night our kids did sleep much better.

This experience was a reminder to me that we must put on the full armor of God and always be alert and ready for battle because Satan likes nothing more than to break up marriages and families and that he will do anything to disrupt our ministries. Remember, he is prowling around like a lion to see who he can devour. We have the power of Christ to overcome the enemy. *"You, dear children are from God and have overcome them, because the one who is in you is greater than the one who is in the world."* 1 John 4:4

Reflection

Spiritual warfare is real. Remember, the enemy will try every way possible to devour you. Put on the full armor of God and stand firm against the evil one. There is power in the name of Jesus.

"The LORD will fight for you; you need only to be still."

Exodus 14:14

Day 18

The Pink Bible

"Rejoice always, pray continually, give thanks in all circumstances; for this is God's will for you in Christ Jesus." 1 Thessalonians 5:16-18

Deeper Reading: Philippians 4

Do you ever think back on something and it just brings a smile to your face? There is a man in the Philippines who carries a pink Bible that brings that smile to my face every time I think of him. We were on a mission trip to the Philippines with our young church plant. This is the church plant that God had given us a vision for to be an Acts 1:8 church and as part of the DNA of the church, we wanted to have a partnership with an unreached people group. We had just launched our first service together in January, and in February we were taking a group of six to the Philippines. One day we were out sharing the gospel and the last home that we came to that day was a man sitting outside his home in a broken plastic chair. We exchanged greetings and he told me that he had always wanted a Bible. All I had was my pink Bible, so I handed it over to him. I shared the gospel with him, and he believed. It was a great moment, and I was so grateful for the opportunity to share with him God's word.

Fast forward five years later. A team from that same church plant went back to the Philippines on another mission trip. While they were there, they went to the local church in the neighborhood where I gave the man my pink Bible. What still amazes me and brings a smile to my face is that one of the guys said he still had his pink Bible and was now involved in the local church.

Reflection

Sometimes, it is easy for us to get down with all the negative stuff going on. Right now, I want you to think of something that puts a smile on your face. *"Finally, brothers and sisters, whatever is true, whatever is noble, whatever is right, whatever is pure, whatever is lovely, whatever is admirable-if anything is excellent or praiseworthy-think about such things."* Philippians 4:8

"May these words of my mouth and this meditation of my heart be pleasing in your sight, LORD, my Rock and my Redeemer."

Psalm 19:14

Day 19

Losing Sarah Beth

"Blessed are those who mourn for they will be comforted."

Matthew 5:4

Deeper Reading: Romans 8:28; Job 1:21

Losing a child is a parent's worst nightmare. The summer of 2016, I experienced what no mother ever wants to experience: giving birth and planning a funeral in the same day.

We had prayed for our 4th child for five years. One of the prayers that we prayed for our child, is that they would be a child that would take the gospel to the ends of the earth. We were all excited about her arrival and as we prayed for her name, God spoke through my son. He sat down one morning for breakfast and said we should name her Sarah Beth. We all felt in our hearts this was the name God wanted us to name her. It was the perfect name for her. Not long after that, God gave me a beautiful dream one night of her beautiful face. She was gorgeous and looked angelic. I told my husband we are in trouble because this child was going to be beautiful. The morning of June 30, 2016, I went in for just a routine checkup. Matt stayed home with the other kids that morning so I could go to the doctor. As I laid there on the exam table to listen to her heartbeat, they could not find one. I was 28 weeks along. I felt numb. I couldn't even think, and with tears flowing down my face, I made it home to tell my family.

That afternoon I went to the hospital to give birth to my child that was already gone. When I held her in my arms, her face was not how I wanted to remember it. I then remembered the dream the Lord gave me about seeing her face. I can still picture it clearly in my head to this day. She was beautiful.

The day of her funeral came and I specifically asked the Lord if he would comfort me through His creation the way he did when my father passed away. After the funeral, my husband and I sat on the front porch together. When we looked up in the sky, there was a rainbow that I knew was just for me. The way He loves on us never ceases to amaze me.

Months after her death, God laid it on our hearts to start a scholarship in honor of her. The scholarship funds someone's first international mission trip. Her precious short life has impacted people all over the world with the gospel.

Reflection

Losing my child was one of the hardest things I have ever had to go through. When we mourn, He comforts us like no one else can. I pray if you have lost someone, that you will cling to Him and feel His amazing love and comfort all around you.

Day 20

Is God Enough?

"Consider it pure joy, my brothers and sisters, whenever you face trials of many kinds, because you know that the testing of your faith produces perseverance." James 1:2-3

Deeper Reading: James 1; 1 John 3-4

Is God enough for me? It's a question that I asked myself the summer of 2016. It's easy to say yes when everything is going great but what about when you face trials of many kinds?

For the first time in my life, I was mad at God and blamed Him for my misery. I looked at God like He was some kind of villain from a Disney movie. I kept hearing the phrase, God is love, God is love, God is love repeated in my mind over and over. I was struggling to look at God as a loving God. I was blaming Him for taking my dad, my daughter, and all the trials that we had encountered in following Him. I actually cursed God for the very first time, but I immediately repented. That voice kept coming over and over, Julie, I am love! So, I finally had to ask the question to myself, is God enough for me in the world? When I go through my worst nightmare here on earth will He be enough for me? The Spirit reminded me as I was praying and reading in His Word that God is enough for me and He loves me more than absolutely anyone. He is my love, redeemer, comforter, protector, provider, counselor, teacher, and the most amazing love that I will ever encounter. He is Enough!

Reflection

God never promised that it would be easy following Him. We will face trials of many kinds but those trials will grow us and there is a loving God that will be right there walking the journey with us. He is enough! He is love. *"You dear children, are from God and have overcome them, because the one who is in you is greater than the one who is in the world."* 1 John 4:4

"He said: "In my distress I called to the LORD, and he answered me. From deep in the realm of the dead I called for help, and you listened to my cry."

Jonah 2:2

Day 21

Healing From Everything

"The prayer of a righteous person is powerful and effective."

James 5:16

Deeper Reading: James 5; 1 Peter 5:10

I need healing! A lot of times when we think of healing, we think of our physical bodies that need healed. It was three weeks after our daughter's funeral and my husband was teaching through James Ch. 5, and I realized that I was sick just not physically, but spiritually. I needed someone to pray over me. I always go to my husband in times like this, but at this time, he was broken as well. I started praying for someone to pray over me, so I could be restored. About a week after I started praying, I received a phone call from a wonderful woman in the faith that invited me to go to a women's leader conference with her. When we got there, we needed to pick the different break out sessions to go to. One of the sessions we chose was one specifically for pastors' wives. When we walked in, my spirit was immediately drawn to the speaker. She asked everyone to share their stories, and I just sat there. There was no way that I wanted to share my story. About three other ladies had gone and then the speaker looked at me and said "I want to hear your story." I was thinking, "oh my goodness, here it goes. Do I think these ladies are ready to hear all I have to say because I am broken?"

Everything came babbling out. When I shared my story, the speaker too had experienced some of the same hardships in ministry. Then I got to the part about losing my daughter; she had lost a daughter also in the exact same way. That woman had walked a journey like mine before me and she knew how to minster to my heart. There were about ten other pastor's wives in that room that day that prayed over me. God gave this woman powerful words to pray over me that no one would have been able to pray unless they have walked in some of my shoes before me. I could feel my spirit starting to heal as they laid hands on me and prayed.

Reflection

There will be times when you are broken and spiritually sick. You will need someone to lay hands on you and pray. When that time comes, seek someone who is stronger in the faith than you and have them pray over you.

Taylor Collins Schnitzler

Day 22

A Time to Rest

"Come to me, all you who are weary and burdened, and I will give you rest." Matthew 11:28

Deeper Reading: Exodus 20:8-10; 33:12-14

We live in such a fast pace world that we really don't take the time to rest. We are constantly running to school functions, meetings, sports practice and games, etc. Before we realize it, we haven't taken anytime to relax and we experience burn-out and exhaustion. God created the Sabbath day for our benefit and made it part of the Ten Commandments. He knew we would need rest from our work. He created the world in six days and took the seventh day to rest. He set us an example.

After our storms in ministry, the hard work of church planting, and losing our daughter, God knew we needed a time of rest. God gave us a sabbatical year. We were still serving, but my husband had a full-time ministry position as a worship pastor and not the lead pastor. My husband and I both love the beach; it is a healing place for us. I grew up going to beach every year as a kid on vacation so it always brings back sweet memories for me. So, God gave us a sabbatical year in Florida close to the beach. We spent so many nights walking the coast at sunset, having picnics, beach days, and my husband found a new love of fishing for salt water fish. It was a time where we could rest and catch our breathes. I am so thankful that God knew we needed this Sabbatical year.

Reflection

Are you in need of a time of rest? God gave us that command for our benefit. We need to take Sabbaths in our lives. Remember, God created the Sabbath day for us. We will need to rest, so we will always be ready for the next assignment.

Amazing Love

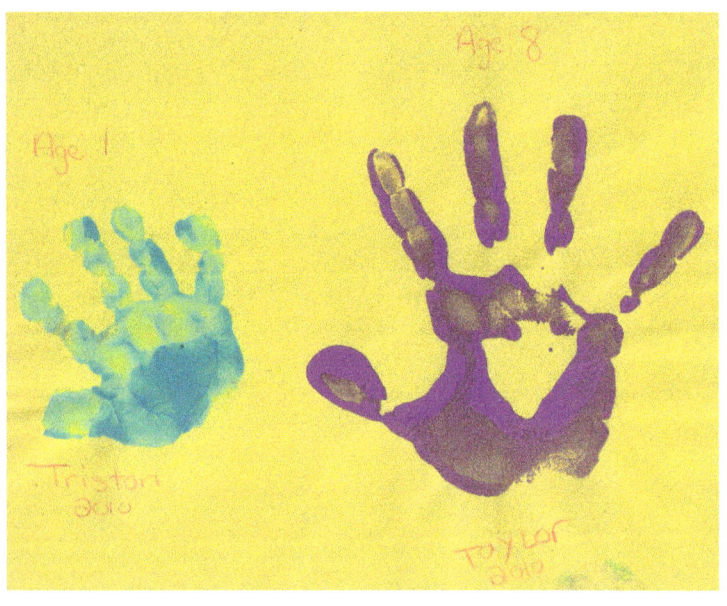

Julie Collins

Day 23
I Need You to Follow Me

"Whoever wants to be my disciple must deny themselves and take up their cross and follow me. For whoever wants to save their life will lose it, but whoever loses their life for me will find it." Matthew 16:24-25

Deeper Reading: Joshua 3; Deuteronomy 28: 1-14; Mark 10: 29-31

Do you think God would ever have you surrender everything to follow Him? Would you be willing to give it all up: your job, your house, your belongings, your wealth? These following words penetrated my heart over and over as God was preparing my heart to follow Him. *"Whoever wants to be my disciple must deny themselves and take up their cross and follow me."* (Matthew 16:24-25)

Our time of rest was over and God was telling us it was time for our next assignment. We knew He wanted us to continue to prepare ourselves for our calling in missions. We knew we were going to have to further our biblical education. The questions we asked were, how and where? We had just bought a brand-new home, the ministry position was easy, and we loved living close to the beach. The Lord asked my husband to resign his position without another job in mind and told him to get his masters degree. (We were thinking, how in the world are we supposed to pay for that?) He wanted me to work on my biblical education also.

"Without faith, it is impossible to please God" (Hebrews 11:6). We felt Him telling us to surrender our job, home, and everything and walk in faith and trust Him. We surrendered and moved to Kentucky for me to work on my biblical education. We still didn't have a clue about a job for Matt, we just knew God told him to get his master's degree. My husband receives service-connected disability and he had just recently started getting 20% because of his knees. He had no idea about this when he resigned, but found out a couple of weeks later that there was a program that would pay for his masters because he had 20% disability but in order for it to work, he had to be unemployed. They not only paid for his degree but gave us money to live off of while he was in school. It's amazing when you walk in obedience and faith, the things God does. I don't know why I ever still

45

doubt. In Joshua Ch. 3 it talks about how God goes before you; we just need to be ready to follow him. He had definitely gone before us and prepared the way.

Reflection

If God asks you to pick up your cross and follow Him, would you? There is nothing easy about the cross, and He said we cannot be His disciple unless we deny ourselves and pick up that cross and follow Him. He may not ask you to leave your home or give up your job, but He could and would you be willing?

"Whoever does not take up their cross and follow me is not worthy of me."

Matthew 10:38

Day 24

God Loves Her More

"Set your minds on things above, not on earthly things. For you died, and your life is now hidden with Christ in God." Colossians 3:2-3

Deeper Reading: Matthew 2

It's hard to think about someone loving your child more than you. We think that we know what's best for them and what they need better than anyone. There is one who loves your child more than you and that is God. When God asked us to surrender to go on a journey with Him while we were in Florida, our oldest was sixteen. She loved the Christian school she was going to and didn't really want to move, although spiritually, she wasn't doing well. I knew where we were going that she would have to go back to homeschooling. I remember thinking, she will not have a high school graduation. I cannot do that to her. The Lord said, "Julie, you are thinking of earthly things and I need you to be kingdom minded." I had been praying for her to be surrounded by followers of Him and people who were chasing after Him in obedience.

In the book of Matthew, the Lord had spoken to Joseph and told him to escape and take Jesus to Egypt to protect him from Herod because Herod would try and destroy him. The enemy has a plan for your children too. God knew what Taylor needed and I just needed to trust that He loved her more and knew what was best for her. He had me take her to a Bible College while I furthered my biblical education. The college is for people who have been called out to serve in ministry. She made really good friends with a few people who were sold out to Christ and wanted to follow Him in obedience and were there training for the ministry. One of those friends ended up becoming her husband and she also surrendered her life to Christ as well.

Reflection

Sometimes, we think we know what's better for our children and what they need. The truth is that God loves your children more. We are raising them for Him. We need to trust Him with them and be obedient to whatever he tells us to do. We need to be willing to take them to Egypt if the Lord needs us to.

"And everyone who has left houses or brothers or sisters or father or mother or wife or children or fields for my sake will receive a hundred times as much and will inherit eternal life."

Matthew 19:29

Day 25

Interceding

"... but he hears the prayer of the righteous." Proverbs 15:29

Deeper Reading: Genesis 18-19; John 17; Philippians 4:6

Have you ever had someone step in and help you when you couldn't help yourself? You thought, I can figure it out and I don't really need help. Maybe we do that because we don't want to burden anyone with helping us or maybe we do it because we think we don't need the help. After each birth of my children, my mom would come and stay with us for a week. She would get up with the baby in the middle of the night and let us sleep. She would cook, clean, and do the laundry. I didn't even know that I would need that but after our first child came, I was forever thankful. Sometimes, we need people interceding and praying for us when we don't even realize we need it.

In Genesis Ch. 18 &19, Abraham is pleading with God about the wicked city of Sodom. Abraham asked God if he found righteous people there would he please not destroy the city. He knew his nephew Lot was living there in that wicked city that had corrupted him and wanted God to rescue him. It is a beautiful story of Abraham interceding and talking to God when Lot was not at a place where he was probably even talking to God. I can relate to Lot. In my teenage years I chose to live a life that was not one of following God but the complete opposite. I am thankful that I had a mom praying for me when I was in rebellion against the Lord during my teenage years. She was praying for God to rescue me. Just like the Lord rescued Lot, He also rescued me because I had someone interceding and praying on my behalf.

Reflection

The story of Abraham praying for Lot is one of the most beautiful showings of intercessory prayer. If there is someone you know that needs rescuing from the sin they are in, I pray that you will intercede for them. *"He hears the prayers of the righteous."* Proverbs 15:29

Day 26

Be Strong and Courageous

"Be Strong and courageous. Do not be afraid; do not be discouraged, for the LORD your God will be with you wherever you go." Joshua 1:9

Deeper Reading: Psalm 112:7; Matthew 14:27; Proverbs 15:29; Psalm 50:15

Just about everyone has some kind of fear of something. For me, I have a fear of mice and snakes. Not everyone has this fear but for me they make me stand on top of furniture if I see a mouse run through the living room. If I see a snake, I usually push my husband into it because I am so scared, which makes him so mad because he is scared of them too. We are a great team when it comes to snakes, we are both running the opposite direction. So, we all have different fears but I pray I never let my fear stop me from being obedient to following God.

God, had just told our family to go to a land to live where we would not know anyone. It was a place where Christians are extremely persecuted and its illegal to go to as missionaries. Over and over in my spirit, He told me to be strong and courageous. We were obedient and went to this foreign country. Two weeks into being in this strange country where we knew absolutely no one, couldn't speak the language or couldn't even call a taxi, our youngest daughter, Emily, came down with a fever and severe leg pain. When her fever wouldn't go away, we had to find a doctor. We found a doctor that had a translator and she sent us to a public Chinese hospital. We were using our phones to help us translate. We also didn't have international insurance, so we had to pay cash up front for the hospital, doctors, lab work, and all other tests. After a week in the hospital, they sent us home and said her fever should go away. The fever and leg pain persisted so we found another doctor. They ran more tests and told us to prepare for the worst. The word cancer came into our vocabulary.

So here we are in a strange country with the overwhelming feeling of extreme culture shock and now our daughter may have cancer. The words, "I feel like someone has punched me in the gut!" came from my husband's mouth. I felt hopeless and then the words *"Take Courage! It is I. Don't be afraid."* (Matthew 14:27) came from His word that filled my heart with a peace in this storm. They sent us to yet another hospital that specializes in children. We were there for yet another week, but I started noticing my child starting to feel better. One morning a group of about 15 doctors walked into our room to talk about the results from the blood work and other testing. They said, "we cannot explain this, but all her bloodwork is normal." They couldn't understand it, but I knew my God had healed her!

Reflection

There will always be something that we fear, but if God asks us to do something we just need to obey and trust Him. He can calm the storm.

"Have I not commanded you? Be strong and courageous. Do not be afraid; do not be discouraged, for the LORD your God will be with you wherever you go."

Joshua 1:9

Day 27

Learning to Love People

"A new command I give you; Love one another. As I have loved you, so you must love one another. By this everyone will know that you are my disciples, if you love one another." John 13: 34-35

Deeper Reading: 1 Corinthians 13

Am I the only one that struggles to love people who are mean especially to my husband or kids? This is probably one of the hardest things for me to do is love on someone who has hurt me, my husband, or my children.

During our family Bible time, we were memorizing 1 Corinthians Ch. 13 as a family. As we meditated on that verse day in and day out, God said," Julie, you have a love problem." Those words were hard to hear, but I knew they were true. I am the type of person who can write people off or push them away easily if I feel they have wronged me or if they have hurt me or my family. However, God convicted me that instead, I must forgive those individuals. What I have learned though, is that it doesn't mean we have to have them over for dinner and play board games together. We are allowed to create boundaries in our lives as a means of protecting ourselves and our families. I am a work in progress with this, but God does tell us to pray for our enemies and bless those that persecute you.

There was a lady that had caused my family much grief and said terrible things about my family. I had hatred in my heart for her. I knew this hatred was affecting my relationship with the Lord. I asked God to help me love her and see her the way He loves her. Two weeks went by after I prayed that prayer, and I saw her at my child's softball game that evening. Nothing in our circumstances had changed but my heart towards her had. I was able to walk up to her and hug her neck and tell her that I loved her. Only God can put that kind of love in my heart towards someone that I do not like. *"Dear children, let us not love with words or speech but with actions and in truth."* (1 John 3:18)

Reflection

Do you have a love problem? Ask God to search your heart and help you to love those that are unlovable. He can and He will. *"But love your enemies, do good to them. And lend to them without expecting to get anything back. Then your reward will be great, and you will be children of the Most High, because he is kind to the ungrateful and wicked. Be merciful, just as your Father is merciful."* (Luke 6:35-36)

Nooh built the Ark.
GOD sent a rainbow
as a promise never
to flood the Earth.

Emily Collins

Day 28

Hearing Him

"The LORD confides in those who fear him; he makes his covenant known to them." Psalm 25:14

Deeper Reading: John 5:30; Psalm 32:8; Hebrews 13:20-21

Do you ever struggle with whether or not you heard the Lord clearly? I think if we are all honest, we will all have listened to those words, "did God really say that?" "He wouldn't ask you to do that." "You're not good enough to do that." These are lies straight from the pit of hell. If God is speaking to you about something it will line up with His word and will not contradict His character.

In the fall of 2011, I was sweeping my floor in the church parsonage that we were living in. I heard God so clearly say to me in my spirit that He wanted me to do something for women. For over ten years I have prayed, searched, waited, doubted, been discouraged, and have even asked the question, "did He even ask me to do that." Fast forward to the spring of 2021. I kept hearing the word "surrender." I thought, God what are you asking me to surrender? I have kept journals for the past 10 years that have included my journey with the Lord. It is my prayers poured out to Him, scripture that has captivated my heart, and how he has spoken to me.

As I continued to pray and seek Him, it became obvious that he was asking me to surrender to write down my journey for Him. Here's the thing, I am no writer. It is probably one of the weakest things about me. But, isn't that just what He wants, to use the weak so He can get the glory for it all? I said, "Oh Lord, I can't do that." Through a Bible Study that I was doing at the time by Priscilla Shrier, He made it clear to me that He had called me to do it. He told me that he would walk with me, equip me, and would put people in my path. My job is to just be obedient.

Reflection

Do you ever struggle with hearing God's voice? Don't listen to the lies of the enemy. When God is speaking to you, you will be able to tell as long as it lines up with scripture, just do it and don't delay. He will walk with you.

"Let the morning bring me word of your unfailing love, for I have put my trust in you. Show me the way I should go, for to you I entrust my life."

Psalm 143:8

Day 29

How Long Will I Be In Prison?

"Now to him who is able to do immeasurably more than all we ask or imagine, according to his power that is at work within us, to him be glory in the church and in Christ Jesus throughout all generations, forever and ever! Amen." Ephesians 3:20-21

Deeper Reading: Genesis 37-41

How long will I be in prison to my calling? That question kept coming back to me. I knew God had told us He wanted us to be overseas. God had given us a wonderful church for my husband to pastor when we evacuated China due to the pandemic in 2020. I just couldn't help feeling like I was sitting in prison to what God had called us to do: How much longer? I thought of the story of Joseph and how God had given him a dream when he was young that his brothers would bow down to him. Then he was betrayed by his brothers, sold into slavery, and then sent to prison. I am sure he too thought, how long will I be in prison before God will show me what I know He has called me to do. I also thought about Paul and while he was in prison, he wrote most of the New Testament.

While I was in prison to my calling, God had me write down my journey. If I did not have that time in prison, I would have not had the opportunity to write down my journey.

Reflection

Do you feel like you're in prison? There are times when we all feel that way. Just like God was with Joseph and with Paul, he is there with you too. He knows the plans that he has for us. We must trust in His love for us that He will work everything out for good, for those that love the Lord. He may need us to be in prison for a while so he can accomplish His will. Less of me and more of Him.

"Wait for the LORD; be strong and take heart and wait for the LORD."

Psalm 27:14

Day 30

The Puzzle Pieces Coming Together

"For I know the plans I have for you, declares the LORD, plans to prosper you and not to harm you, plans to give you hope and a future."
Jeremiah 29:11

Deeper Reading: Isaiah 42:6-7; John 13:7

Do you ever wonder how God will use all that you have been through? How will he put all the pieces of the puzzle together? We have longed to be permeant overseas since we have felt God calling us into ministry in 2007. The Lord has had us pastoring churches, church planting, and even serving as a worship and mission pastor in the mainland United States. God did use us as semester missionaries a couple of times but we always desired for it to be permanent. To others, we always seemed discontent but that longing would not go away to be overseas.

Then after fifteen years of wondering, the puzzle pieces started coming together. We knew God was telling us it was time and that He wanted us overseas. It would be on an island on the other side of the world. Could this really be happening? All these little things God would give us along the way like," I want you overseas", "I want you to be on an island", "I want you to work with women," all these pieces of the puzzle were put together in matter of months. The thing we had been waiting for, dreaming of, and being called to was finally happening. We were finally going to be overseas.

Reflection

Do you ever wonder how God is going to put everything together? Do you wonder how it will work out? I am sure we all have these questions. One thing I know is true, is that His love for us is everlasting and as long as we follow Him in obedience to do His will, our desires will be His desires. He will give us the desires of our heart.

Day 31

Remembering What God Has Done

"I will remember the deeds of the Lord; yes, I will remember your miracles of long ago." Psalm 77:11

Deeper Reading: Philippians 4:4-9

When you think of the things that God has done for you, what comes to your mind? When the shepherds had just visited Jesus after he was born, Mary treasured all those things in her heart and pondered on them. She had seen God do amazing things like become pregnant with God's son while she was a virgin, had an angel speak to her, and shepherds told her of what God had shown them and where to find Jesus. She wanted to remember all those things in her heart. When I think about all that God has done for me, it fills me with such joy and causes me to praise Him. There are times when I want to dwell on the bad, but I am reminded of this verse: *"Finally, brothers and sisters, whatever is true, whatever is noble, whatever is right, whatever is pure, whatever is lovely, whatever is admirable- if anything is excellent or praiseworthy-think about such things."* (Philippians 4:8-9).

When I look back on my walk with Jesus so far, I still remember the rejections, loss, betrayal, isolation, and other hurts, but when I look and see how God brought me through those things and how He walked beside me, I throw my hands up in praise and awe of Him. So, for instance when I look back and remember the things God has done for me, I think about Him rescuing me from my sins, giving me gifts when I didn't deserve them, take me away to isolated places so I could hear him , bring healing to me when I was broken, break my heart for people, leading me to them on the other side of the world, healing my daughter, walking along beside me when I felt so rejected by others, and watching my kids give their life to Him. These are just a few treasures over the years that I want to store up and remember all the things He has done.

Reflection

What are the treasures that you want to store up in your heart. I pray when you remember all the wonderful things God has done for you that it will cause you to praise Him and tell others of the things He has done.

"But seek ye first the kingdom of God, and his righteousness; and all these things shall be added unto you. "

Matthew 6:33

The Lord appeared to us in the past, saying:

"I have loved you with an

everlasting love;

I have drawn you with

unfailing kindness."

Jeremiah 31:3

www.ingramcontent.com/pod-product-compliance
Lightning Source LLC
Chambersburg PA
CBHW051646120626
46551CB00015B/2234